Into the Land of Me

Into the Land of Me

*By
Charlie*

Copyright © 2009 by Maggie Scrobonia, OTR/L
All rights reserved. No part of this book may be reproduced in any form without permission in writing from the publisher.

Red Rooster Publishing
Healdsburg, California
www.redroosterpublishing.com

Red Rooster Publishing is committed to providing quality books that inspire and entertain those who read them.

Cover Design: Janet Meadows
J.C.Meadows Photography

Edited by: Meg Hamill
www.meghamill.com

ISBN – 0982590903
EAN 13 - 9780982590904
Printed in the United States of America

Acknowledgements

First and foremost, to my loving husband Michael. Your endless patience, financial support and ability to "let it go," have allowed me to step into my place of power. Without you, this work would not have come to fruition.

To my children, David and Alex, for allowing me to read these stories to you, over and over and over, during the last two years. Thank you for your continued encouragement and love.

To Katie, for all the times when you sat at my feet, sharing your never ending, unconditional love, when no one else was around.

To my sister Judy, my best friend and my muse. Without you, I would not have considered turning my "therapy" into a book.

To my editor Meg Hamill, for your incredible editing skills. Your thoughts, insights and endless corrections made this work complete.

To Janet Meadows for creating the perfect cover design. I so admire your incredible photography skills.

And last, but not least to my friends who have supported me throughout this process. You will never know the depth of love and gratitude I have for you all. Dalene, Dot, Gisela, Catherine and Bridgette thank you for your honest input and encouragement, and Kim thank you for allowing me to share a little about you with the readers.

Preface

My father had a wonderful gift that allowed him to predict the sex of all of his children. One after another, the names of my siblings were selected prior to their births, and all of them were correct…except for mine. I was to be named Charles Andrew Hall— Hence, Charlie. You see, it was on this hot, August day that my father's 20-year track record broke and I arrived— Margaret Ann Hall, instead.

All of my life, I have never had just one name. Some of my siblings and their friends call me Charlie. My parents for the most part called me Margie—except when I was in trouble; then it was Margaret Ann.

As I grew up and went to high school, my friends started to call me Mag or Mags. A boyfriend in college called me Magpie and I even had one dear friend call me Mad-dog.

As I grew and matured, somehow Mags turned into Maggie. Now I can't have my family call me Maggie; it's just plain weird, and I can't stand it when my husband or my current friends try to call me Margie.

So when it came time to think about the "Author" of this book, I chose Charlie. It is after all, plain, simple and easy to remember (especially when telling everyone you know about this great book you just read).

Also, more to the point, I felt it was highly symbolic. The meaning of the name "Charles" is "free man." The name encompasses a lot about me and how I live my life—doing what I want, when I want and how I want. That's not always good, but it *is* quite "freeing." I also wanted to honor the spirit in which the name was originally intended. My parents, like most parents, had great insight as to who I would one day become. Even though I turned out to be a gender surprise, they really knew my core spirit way before I had the opportunity to blossom. I'm sure during my teen years, they wished that they had named me Katherine, which means "pure..." but, oh well.

Well, there you go, just a little something for you to better understand me (and my twisted psyche) before you enter *Into the Land of Me*. Welcome.

Sleep Deprivation: Viewing Life Through Eyes Half Closed

I am an expert on sleep deprivation, though I have no formal training other than living day to day with substandard sleep. The idea for this book came to me as I was standing in the shower (actually, sitting because I was too pooped to stand). As I pondered why I felt so empty, and so out of balance, it hit me—I was absolutely and chronically, exhausted. It occurred to me then that exhaustion, like the water running over my body, also ran over me. Not in a soothing way either. More like a truck running over a Twinkie on a very busy freeway. It was at that moment, the realization came; I had been in this psychotic place before, actually many times before. But there was something about finally *seeing* this pattern clearly for what it was that actually awakened me (well at least just a little) and made me pay attention. I sat there wondering "Why me? Why can't I just get good night's sleep?"

That morning began like so many others. I am the mother of two teenagers, I own my own business and I "sleep" (we'll use that term lightly) with a wonderful man with Restless Leg Syndrome. I had just taken the kids to school and had experienced an explosive episode of Road Rage. I was so proud of myself for yelling at a woman who was cautiously waiting to cross the crosswalk as two cars inched their way toward her. My thirteen-year-old son, who had been awake until 2:00 a.m. finishing a report, was actually trying to calm *me* down. "Mom, chill…it's OK." (For those of you without teenagers, this is not normal behavior. Usually it's the other way around.)

Now, I am not one to whine for long, but at eight in the morning, after very little sleep and a long day ahead of me, the thought of having a big old pity party was looking pretty good. I could either drop to the ground and sob my eyes out or I could take the bull by the horns and give it a good fight. So that morning after my road rage I went home to get some clarity. Here's what I came up with: I truly believe that we are all given these struggles and challenges for a reason. We may not like what the universe has handed us, but if we pay attention, we can grow and learn and even benefit from them. So that is exactly what I intend to do. In the pages that follow I'm going to take the bull by the horns and explore this thing from the inside out. Fierce Grace has come to me in the form of sheer exhaustion, but I have a hunch there's something more there to be seen. Hopefully I can stay awake long enough for that to happen.

Motherhood: Look Who's Napping Now

*B*ack when my children were little, I was blessed with the option of being a stay-at-home mom. In hindsight, it really was for the best, as I'm sure I would have accidentally killed one of my kids if I'd had to balance work and child rearing all at once. One of my first, memorable moments in the Land of Sleep Deprivation (LSD), occurred when my children were around four and two years of age. (Notice I say "around," as the concept of time really is a blur.) Anyway, I think I was going on four years with little to no sleep. Being the wonderful wife and mom that I am, I chose not to interrupt my husband's sleep, because after all, he did have to leave the house each day to go to work. (I know, I know…that's a whole separate book waiting to be written: *How To Be a Stay-at-Home Mom Who Does Nothing but Eat Bon Bons and Sleep All Day.*) Anyway, back to my memorable moment in LSD. I would never have expected what happened next. On this particular, bright and sunny day, I decided that a trip into town was just what we all needed.

I had both kids in the car, buckled in nice and safe. We were driving through town when all of the sudden my four-year-old son began to scream. In his outburst I did not hear the "I'm-Pissed-Get-Me-Out-of-This-Car-Seat" scream, but rather I heard the "Oh-My-God-Something-is-Killing-Me" scream. Trust me, there is a difference. So, with no sleep, nerves frazzled and panic running through my veins, I drove directly to my doctor's office and somehow we all made our way inside. By now, all three of us were sobbing and I can honestly say that at that point, I had "lost it." Gotta love living in a small town where, when you're freakin' out at the doctor's office, you actually get bumped to the front of the line. The diagnosis was not good: I was officially a nut job. I left with a prescription that read: "Dear Mr. S., You are on duty for the next two nights. Your wife needs to sleep." So, with two healthy children in tow and my sample sleeping pills in my purse, I stumbled home for a rest.

A Trip to the Land "Down Under"

I can't remember what it feels like to be rested. I do however, know what it feels like to pollute your system with stimulants in order to try to get through the next several hours. That is my current system for survival. Go ahead, I dare you to ask: "How's that workin' for ya?" because my reply will be a sharp, "Oh shut up." You see, I have discovered that in LSD (Land of Sleep Deprivation—in case you are too tired to remember) there is a place called "Crabby Town." I travel there frequently. I believe that I have the potential to be one of the major investors in this toxic place.

Let's take a quick detour to "Crabby Town" (CT) where no one can do anything right, where everything smells funny and God forbid if you're a man. In CT (remember, abbreviations are important when you're too tired to speak), dogs and cats scatter about in front of you, not running from immediate danger, but intuitively taking cover in case the volcano erupts. There are three major food sources in CT: pre-made frozen dinners, macaroni and cheese and cereal. If you expect to find something different, you are putting yourself in grave danger and entering into the "seriously stupid" category. While visiting CT, a whole new light is shed on the phrase "duck and cover!" And no, that's not what's for dinner!

Driving in LSD is not an easy thing to do. You almost need a special license to drive "under the influence" of exhaustion. Stop signs tend to be more difficult to maneuver, especially when given a choice to turn right or left. Today during one of my many trips into town, I had a run-in with one of those signs. Right …? Left …? What's a girl to do? So, like any good zombie, I chose to delay the decision awhile, pass through the stop sign and wait in the middle of the street until it became clear what to do next. What the hell…I honestly couldn't remember which way to turn. Eventually, the left turn won. Just in case you were curious.

Pedestrians aren't nice in LSD. I think most of them are transplants from Crabby Town; I have not met one nice one in the last three days. I have several issues with these crabs. First, they have no appreciation for quick stops made by my car, halfway in the middle of a crosswalk. Do you know how much skill it takes, as a driver, to snap out of a daze and stop a speeding car? Second, they certainly don't enjoy playing "Beat the Light." It's as if they are afraid to put a little sprint in their steps to get from the green "go" hand to the flashing "don't-do-it-ding-dong" light. No fun at all! Third, these transplants don't know how to accept an apology after almost being run over. They do, however, have excessive stiffness in their middle fingers as I've seen on multiple occasions in the last several days. Not a pleasant place to live.

You Go Girl...

*I*t's now 10:00 p.m. and everyone is asleep or heading to bed. Here's the interesting thing…I'm not joining them. I have officially polluted my system full of sugars, caffeine and drugs, and this particular combination of stimulants have somehow generated enough energy in my body to drag this day on a little bit longer. For what, I don't know. I sit in front of the TV clicking the channels around and around, seemingly searching for something to shut me off. I have a wonderful mattress, a comfortable room, and even a good book waiting for me, yet I sit here trying to decompress. I don't know how to stop. I don't know when to stop. Step #1: When tired all day long, go to bed when everyone else does, or before, if you need to. Nighty Night.

C

I find it interesting that yesterday was Wednesday January 9, 2007. I realize now in fact, that it was not. I suppose another benefit of living in LSD, is the potential for living by a pretend calendar. You see, today is actually Thursday January 11, 2007. No big deal, just thought someone should know.

Will You Still Love Me Tomorrow?

Last night did not bring the beautiful sleep fairy with her wand and magical sleeping powder. Instead it brought one loyal black lab named "Katie" who slept on the floor next to the couch, unfortunately, next to me. We don't own a big, fluffy, comfy couch; it is more like a brown, leather slope. Don't get me wrong, I'm not ungrateful and I hold no ill will towards it. As my mom used to say, "It is what it is." I do, however, feel that this couch, my newly found "unsleeping" companion, needs a name. As I sit here looking at its fine, overstuffed arms, the round rolls to the foot recliner, the wrinkles and dips and pockets, I immediately think of Larry the Cable Guy. Larry it is. I'm sure as time goes on Larry and I will become intimate friends.

Vacation: Into the Land of Tranquility

When you're exhausted, the first thing you think of is a tropical vacation. After all, what better way to recoup, revive and regenerate than relaxing by the ocean in paradise? So, off to Mexico we went. Warm, crystal-blue water, 85-degree weather, beautiful Cabana Boys offering me fruit by the poolside. I was definitely onto something. How I would pack this tropical paradise into my suitcase and bring it all home, I didn't know, but it was certainly something to ponder between the Margaritas and Piña Coladas.

Our first sunset was a glorious, orange/red fireball that illuminated the sky, slowly fading into purples, pinks and soft, blue-grey hues. Then, all hell broke loose. The Mexican Mosquito Squad came from nowhere, dive-bombing ankles, arms and legs. These highly trained biters actually could maneuver their stingers and bite through socks; we were all quite impressed. Slap, slap, hit, hit, itch, itch, we needed some protection, and fast. As I slathered on this tube of skin saver that came highly recommended from the locals, my first thought was, "Oh, this is really nice, it's not greasy and it has a lovely scent. I really *am* in paradise." 24 hours later, I had a different thought. "Oh my God. I'm on fire! I've been rolled in poison oak and set on fire!" Yup, you guessed it, a lovely allergic reaction had joined my R&R vacation. I was now officially banned from seeing my Cabana Boys. Out went the bikini and on went layers of wraps and a broad-rimmed hat. I was a stunning mummy (pun intended), if I do say so myself. I spent the rest of the week admiring those beautiful, bronze bodies from afar, dreaming of the day I would feel rested and relaxed.

When traveling to Mexico, the one thing you don't want to hear is a knock on the bathroom door from "Mr. Tourista." Well, guess who came knocking the day before we were to head back home. I yelled to my husband, "NO! NO! Don't open the door!" But it was too late, the end was near; death had indeed come a calling. Without sharing all our intimate, gory details, I will say this: If you are weak in the digestive department, think twice before running off to Mexico for a relaxing retreat. Chances are you may spend more time recuperating at home then rejuvenating on the beach.

I love Oprah. She often has these brilliant words of wisdom that will catch my attention. While I lay in bed, dreaming of my long lost Cabana Boys, I remembered something that I had seen on one of her shows. I won't even try to paraphrase her; I'll just give you the gist of what flashed through my exhausted head. It was something along these lines: If you take your strongest characteristic and put it towards service to others, that is when your life begins to turn around. I was definitely in the mood for a 180.

So there I lay, weak and fuzzy and pondering what the hell I was meant to do with my life. How could I best serve others? Granted, this may not have been the most opportune time to plan the rest of my life, but at least it would prove to be entertaining. There were too many choices: healer, writer, counselor, business woman, body builder, stripper—oh the beauty of "dehydration delirium." I could even be Tinker Bell! Seriously! I could move to LA and live in Disneyland and be Tinker Bell! God I love Oprah. I may need to consider this a little while longer, but don't worry, I'll keep you posted.

Watch Out Young Man

Never criticize an exhausted woman once she has made you a meal. If the meat is dry, choke it down. If the potatoes are lumpy, add your own milk. If you decide you no longer like a brand of cereal, I highly suggest you either throw it out when no one is looking or give it to the dog. Whatever you do, you'd better not complain. This one simple act can cause what we call a "homicidal/suicidal reaction" that could result in the loss of life or limb in seconds flat. My husband of 15 years, bless his heart, hasn't figured this one out yet. He likes to live life dangerously, often informing me of likes and dislikes once the meal has been prepared and placed in front of him. Now in most marriages this really isn't a problem—the sharing of likes and dislikes. It's only when one person is totally psychotic (that would be me) that things get ugly. Watch out Bruce Lee and Walker Texas Ranger—your "turn, kick punch" has nothing on me, after being told that the fine-looking sirloin burger I just whipped up special, is overcooked.

Another quick note on my husband; when I say he lives life dangerously, I'm serious. This is a man who can climb anything quickly and gracefully. Yosemite's Half Dome without cables—no problem. 30-foot trees with a running chain saw in one hand—equally smooth. Ban saws, radial saws, hold-in-your-hand saws, zip, zip, zip. The man loves his power tools.

I remember one crisp winter day, under clear blue skies, I looked out the window into our back yard and saw my four-year-old son happily swinging in his plastic, red airplane tree swing. It really was a Kodak moment—and I do mean "moment." As I gazed up to the canopy of the "fruitless mulberry," my jaw dropped and my temper flew. I could not believe what I was seeing. There in the top of the tree was my husband with his chain saw, pruning branches all around my little pilot's head. Our solution was less than desirable—one Social Services surely would have frowned upon: a bicycle helmet, and pruning confined to the backside of the tree. Sometimes a well-rested individual has more persuasive powers over the sleep-deprived. You better watch out.

Creativity Abound!

I've discovered that sleep-deprived people are actually quite creative. We have an amazing ability to make up new uses for common, everyday items. Here's a few of my favorites: locking your car door by aiming and clicking your cell phone, answering the TV remote control, opening your front door by pointing and clicking your car keys, using Desitin (that creamy, diaper rash paste) for toothpaste, opening your front door when the oven timer goes off, using the local phonebook as a cookbook, using a cool oven for storing a fresh carton of milk, using hairspray for deodorant, and clicking your car keys to open the freezer door at the supermarket. Have others? Go ahead, share them with us. Who knows, maybe one of them will catch on and become the next new "craze." Send your ideas to mag@akacharlie.com with the subject heading as: *Creative SD Moves.* Thanks ever so much!

Could This Be Genetic?

*A*fter talking to my sister, it occurred to me that there might be a genetic predisposition to this SD state of being. Much to my surprise, she began speaking LSD (in this case it stands for "Language of the Sleep-Deprived"). Phrases like, "Huh?" and "What?" and "Oh yeah, what'd you just say?" came rolling off her tongue. Finally, someone who spoke my language! I think it must be a female dominant trait as I do have recollections of my mother carrying on with a "deer-in-the-headlights" sort of look. Of course that could have been purely coincidence, as she raised five kids with a 20-year age span between the first and the last. My mom was 40 when she was given the glorious news that I was on the way. Sending the first one off to college and filling the space with a new little screamer, I'm sure made her day. Boy, if I found out now that I was increasing my "case load," there sure would be hell to pay. At that point in the game there would only be one person to blame, and it wouldn't be me! No wonder growing up I often heard, "It was the milkman's fault" or "Well, it could have been the golf instructor," and the classic, "It must have been the pharmacist who passed out placebos instead of birth control pills..." I think my father was just too smart to jump right in and take responsibility for this one.

Physiologically Speaking...

So here's the deal. I wake up this morning, not really knowing what the day is, but aware that it is somewhere around the end of January. The first thing I do is go to my planner, look for today's date, and discover that I have a nine o'clock appointment scheduled. I tend to all my personal tasks, load myself into the car and drive 20 minutes to my first appointment. So proud of myself that I actually arrived promptly, I run up to the door only to find it locked. I take a deep breath, relax and sit down to patiently wait. And I wait. After 15 minutes I place a phone call, "Hi, it's me. I've been waiting for about 15 minutes, but the door is locked. Are you almost here?" And then the bomb hits. "Um, Maggie? Today is Tuesday, not Wednesday. Our appointment is scheduled for Wednesday at nine." Oh—that can't be right...(paper shuffle, organizer opening, day locating...) Crap. "I'm so sorry. I must be losing my mind. I looked at my schedule twice this morning. Well, I guess I'll see you tomorrow!"

That's how this day has begun. As I sit here pondering whether it is a visual or cognitive problem that I can't read my planner, it becomes blatantly clear; it's this darn old SD issue again. This sucker invades every part of your being. It permeates every little cell in your body, grows annoying tentacles that reach up through your synapses— deprogramming the initial signal, then transmitting something totally bogus—just to screw with you. Now how unfair this that?

What Will Your Lover Do For You?

I have begun a very romantic relationship with "Larry," my couch. We have had three glorious evenings together touching, hugging and rolling around in the sack, otherwise known as a sleeping bag. Before this quick romance began, I decided I would not accept Larry as he was, but like any good woman, began to transform him into the sexy, supportive object I knew he could be. Our adventures began around 10:00 p.m. with a mini makeover. Larry definitely needed a new look and feel if this was going to work. For our first evening I chose a lovely blue and red "tuck in" bag that included a small pillow for extra support. Once the bag was laid out lengthwise it was firmly tucked into his crack (come on guys…get your mind out of the gutter), then partially zipped up 1/3 of the way, leaving plenty of room for a seductive stretch. The second evening this look was enhanced by the use of a fashionable, fluffy Temper-Pedic pillow for Larry, two earplugs and a scrumptious, thick robe for me. The third night, all bets were off. Larry had been stuffed, tucked, fluffed, padded, kicked, yelled and cursed at, as the expected improvements refused to appear. Just like a man!

When the Universe Speaks… You Better Listen!

I think the Gods have been testing my sense of humor the last several months. You see, after I began writing this book, I became very rested. I had nothing interesting to share, nothing that resembled SDC's (Sleep Deprivation Characteristics). I felt no desire to purge my soul to the universe at large. Larry and I separated and I began to see life through well-rested, functional glasses. My mother always used the phrase "never look a gift horse in the mouth." As usual, she was right. Things got complicated again somewhere between the bright idea to "grow my therapy business" and the other bright idea to take a "beautiful Sedona vacation."

I had scheduled to take a weeklong course in beautiful Sedona. The family was coming along to enjoy the sun and majestic, red rocks. (Does this sound familiar? Mexico Trip ringing a bell?) In hindsight, there were multiple signals warning me not to go, the likes of which I will never overlook again. It started with the dreams—me in a car, always going downhill very fast and sometimes crashing into walls. Other times the car would have to choose a road and I always took the one pointing downhill. Dreams of stairs, all going down, down, down. Uh, Duh… The *first* signal was the stolen credit card number that we discovered on Thursday, four days before we were to leave. Some destitute person was trying to get a hot date at our expense. Charges from Match.com, Singles.com, and multiple other dating sites, all led us to close the credit card account. Warning number *two* was the failed attempt by the bank to Fed Ex our new cards to us. We delayed our departure waiting for the cards to come and then later found out that the bank had neglected to send them to us at all. Number *three* came when my daughter developed an illness and needed to be put on an antibiotic (four days prior to our departure). As she became worse, not better, we discovered that we needed to change the antibiotic to something stronger. Flashing red light number *four* arrived on Saturday, the day of departure. As we were loading everyone in the car, my daughter said, "My leg hurts…and I itch everywhere."

At this point, my stress level maxed out. I started to get a clue, but in the end chose to ignore it. I even began to voice my hesitation out loud, "Maybe this is a sign that we shouldn't go," I offered. "Maybe I am not meant to take this course," to which my husband replied, "Are you kidding?" Maybe I was just experiencing good old fashioned fear of the unknown. All would be fine after one quick stop at the pediatrician's office, and then off we'd go. "Happy trails to you…"

Again, I'll spare you from the details of traveling with a dreadfully sick kid for fourteen hours in a car, and I won't bitch to you about a really gross hotel room in Barstow. Instead, I will jump straight to the scene of the crash…solid red stop light number *five*. After arriving in Sedona on Sunday, talking to our doctor all the while as we traveled across the states, Monday morning, all time stood still. We found ourselves sitting in the emergency room in Sedona trying to schedule an emergency medical flight home. The diagnosis was grim. Hepatitis? Leukemia? A lot of unanswered questions awaited us. Nothing more mattered except my baby, my sweet little "Mander B."

We are blessed. From this nightmare we have gained access to insight and strength we didn't know that we had, and new pathways are opening up for us day by day. Fortunately, we have a somewhat happy ending. My daughter's illness turned out to be a severe allergic reaction to the antibiotic. She is still a very sick little puppy, however, we are expected to have a full recovery, in due time. So, here I am again. Four weeks with little to no sleep. Hmm…maybe the universe wants me to write after all.

Sometimes You Just Have to Go With the Flow

*E*ver have one of those moments when you seriously believe that you just can't take it anymore? I can tell you that I'm becoming quite experienced in knowing when these moments are coming and when I need to start running. Yesterday it all began, the opening of the floodgates, so to speak. Mander B (my daughter's code name) and I have been together now 24/7 for four weeks. To say that she is sick of me is an understatement. Between her pain and my fear, we are quite the riveting couple. We had a very crabby day yesterday. We were like two caged tigers, hungry and ready to pounce at anything. Actually, we really *were* hungry, as I have not made grocery shopping a priority. And the pounce—well, we'll just chock that up to woman's prerogative. After many hours of attempted pain management and pointless snacking, she and I gave up. To different ends of the house we went. For the moment, all was calm and we anxiously awaited the arrival of Dad and Big Brother, to add some happy energy to our sour mix.

With great anticipation and excitement we heard the car pull up, the house door open, then boom…in walks my son with a scowl on his face and a huge fat lip, compliments of a head-on collision with a baseball. Luckily, all the braces remained intact. The lip and the human spirit however, were quite injured. Now in the grand scheme of things, this bump was minor, unless of course you were sleepless, and had been on house arrest as long as I had been. I felt the curtains close over my eyes and the familiar "deer in headlights" look cross over me. I was checking out. Scrambling for any excuse to leave the house, I found a DVD to return to the rental store, grabbed my keys and out I ran. I drove around town, cruising the neighborhood, sunroof open and music blasting. I stopped to pick up some Hot Tamales but had no cash…damn. I needed my sugar fix, just a little high to get me back home. No luck. I would need to be tough and return to duty. Plain and simple, I had no more excuses to stay away from home. I had to go back and finish this. I needed to see it through.

Sleep did come eventually that night, but I awoke with a dream about gardening and snakes, blue and black snakes…on my hands. I don't like snakes, not awake or in my sleep. Screams came, arms flailed, and out of bed I jumped. It must be time to wake up anyway—5:30 a.m.

I do the old timer's morning shuffle. Scratch here, rub there, bouncing my way down the hall to the coffee pot, but something is different today. There is a strange, hissing noise coming from the far end of the house. Like Sherlock Holmes, I gently creep around the corner to discover the unsolved mystery: my handsome, 50-gallon fish tank (yes, that's right, 50…the big five-O) is slowly leaking out onto my carpeted floor. I open the cabinet, grab the hose and start screaming…"Help! Wake up! Help!!!…" I yell this over and over at the top of my lungs. No response. All four family members (that includes my trusty Labrador) continue to enjoy their beauty sleep as I slowly drown in fish water in our TV room. "Get up! Somebody help!" 10 gallons later, some buckets arrive and my three, trusty family members come to my rescue. Now notice I say three family members. One is missing—the one whom I depend upon for so many things. Throughout all of this commotion and my yells for help, this member continues to snooze, big time, dreaming of better places, and grabbing beauty sleep by the handfuls.

Moral of this story? When you are in need of help, you better yell: "TREAT BONE! TREAT BONE!" Then you may, just *may*, see your trusty, lazy, Labrador protector come to your rescue.

It Must Be Time For a Cocktail

I don't have much of a sense of humor this morning, although I have been given a clear message that it is vital to acquire one if I'm going to survive all of this. I have had a total of four hours of sleep and am now pumping caffeine into my system, in a desperate attempt just to be human. I'm hoping God provides me with some good material today, otherwise you may end up tossing this book into your garbage, and that just wouldn't be very nice. So God, what's my line? What am I suppose to share with this gracious audience, that will have them rolling around on the floor splitting a gut? Hmm? Can't hear you...You'd better slap a good one on me cuz I'm just not feeling the spirit today. Amen.

I'm sure you have all heard the phrase, "Be careful what you ask for." This was another of my mother's favorites. Well, I am here to attest to the strength of this concept. I finally get it. I have had my Aha moment! God, or the powers that be, seems to take things quite literally. I asked for a "slap," and what a whopper I got. I am now a believer! At about one o'clock in the afternoon, as I waited to be inspired to write something brilliant for you all, the big one hit. All of the sudden, I felt as if someone had taken a spear and driven it straight through my chest. Yep, I was sure I was having a heart attack. Thank God I had a friend here with me to drive me to the doctor's. Crap, I really didn't have time for this. I still had my daughter home sick, I was in the middle of rearranging the furniture in my house, I had my son at school waiting to be picked up and then taken to his baseball game one hour later, and I had a client scheduled in the middle of all of it. There just wasn't time for this nonsense.

As I sat in the ER, hooked up to monitors and having my blood sucked out of me, the only thing I came up with was…I just don't have time for this. I suppose it's not the best sign when you don't make time to review your life, even as it's passing before your eyes. I believe that is a clear indicator that your life is way…and I mean *way*…out of balance.

Many thanks to those admirable nurses who made multiple trips to my bedside, allowing me the use of their phones. After several phone calls I managed to arrange childcare, rebook my appointment and find a ride home. (My house however, remains in a state of disarray.) In the end, I received a clean bill of health and a "gastric cocktail" via IV. "Don't you have anything better you can add to my IV?" I asked, "Ya know, a little "mellow cocktail" to send me on my way?" I don't believe they all had the same sense of humor I did. Oh well, like I said, I now get it!

Is That Light I See Between the Slits of My Eyes?

I'm sorry to say that I need to change the mojo of this book. If I choose to write about all the unfortunate things that happen to me in my life, I now understand that that's what the universe will provide for me. I proclaim here and now that there will be no more sleep-deprived tragedies or traumas shared here. I just don't have the strength for more material. So, off I go to manifest breathtaking, fun and exciting things that bring peace, light and joy. Come on…don't you think I can find something interesting to write about without me risking life or limb?

Things I want to manifest: winning the lotto, perfect health and an attractive, sexy body. Oh yes…and some good, deep sleep.

Sleep Deprivation or Estrogen Depletion? Menopause is Here to Stay

As the weeks and months have passed, I find myself slipping in and out of self-awareness, partly because of lack of sleep, and partly because of this profound sense of self that is starting to emerge. My desire to change and transform has taken on a life all its own. I compare this mindset to the emergence of a beautiful monarch butterfly cracking through its comfortable cocoon, preparing to expand its wings and fly; or probably more accurately, to that of a schizophrenic.

I have now come to the harsh realization that not only am I exhausted, but I am also smack dab in the middle of menopause—Jekyll and Hyde, hot and cold, sharp and smooth, sleepless, restless and no winning lottery ticket to soften the blow. I don't know if my symptoms are related to living in the LSD or if I'm entertaining a new friend, ED (Estrogen Depletion). Either way, it is now that I need a little of that Fierce Grace I found in the shower when all this started.

Living with ED is almost as dysfunctional as living in LSD. ED however, sheds a new light on things. It was ED that seemed to be the catalyst for this midlife transformation that I felt emerging. This transformation did not come as I expected. I did not immediately fly away with my beautiful new wings. Instead, I crashed first. Big time. So, in honor of this life-altering event, I have created the *Survivors Sister Series:*

Edmanohpause: Is This the Island of Doom?
(Pronounced: Ed-Man-Oh-Pause!)

Krusty the Freak Clown Shows Her Ugly Side. This is the tale of chaos in the circus and how the angry clown succumbs to her own death. In this story, Krusty, who is overwrought, exhausted, angry and just plain mean, begins to understand the impact of emotions on physical health and wellness. As she journeys through the various rings in the circus of her life, she struggles to maintain and juggle all those necessary, daily tasks. Walking the tight rope high above the crowd, she slips and falls, and watches herself slowly tumble toward her impending doom.

(OK, here's the real scoop: perimenopause is obviously a real killjoy to one's sense of well being. When you add being out of balance to the mix, there is just no way to manage walking that fine line we all must walk in our daily lives. It's as if someone starts

shaking the rope from one end. No matter what you do, you just can't balance yourself, and so you fall. As I became angry and resentful about issues in my life, those emotions started to display themselves in my physical being. I still functioned, still performed all of my daily tasks, but with no enjoyment or passion. I had definitely lost my footing.)

Burning Desire—Sex? Who cares! In this tragic comedy our heroine, Daisy, begins to acknowledge that she no longer feels like a beautiful, spring bouquet, but rather feels more like a dried up, drooping, weeping, wilting flower. The desire for sleep strongly overpowers the need for pleasure and thus she struggles to maintain her sanity, and her marriage. Not even her best friend Bob can help her out of this quandary.

(As we all know, the female "flower essence," that good old estrogen, is what makes our libido bloom. Mine of course, dried up like last month's carnations. I think a lot of women at this stage try to add preservative into their "water" rather than just tossing the flowers out. I however, being totally depleted and exhausted, opened the garbage can and dumped the whole bunch in...Gave up, quit, not interested, ka-put. Now, who the heck is this Bob? Well, in honor of all my girl friends who have made this portion of my journey bearable, it will remain our personal joke. God bless my girl friends!)

The Game of Life—The Memoirs of a Menopausal Woman. In the first story of the trilogy, Joan, the main character, is a game show contestant attempting to work her way up the "Golden Functional Ladder." In round one, she plays "Beat the Heat," knowing the signs and symptoms of a hot flash. This is a simple game where the goal is to limit as many ER visits for irregular heartbeats as possible, while not being arrested for indecent exposure. In level two, Joan attempts to read and understand time in the popular show of, "What Time is it Anyway?" This is sleep deprivation's version of "Whose Line is it Anyway?" Moving up to level three, she begins to see the challenges and struggles in this relationship brain teaser of "Are you Kidding Me!?" a very complicated mix of "Jeopardy" and "Family Feud" co-hosted by the lovely, Ms. Mood Swing. Next, Joan's physical strength and endurance are challenged in this difficult maze of "Health/No Health," a kick ass game of "Deal/No Deal," where multiple briefcases are loaded with symptoms of mysterious origin. Only one case contains the path to true health. Making the right choice is the key to regaining her strength. And finally, "The Choice is Right." Decisions abound in this final, cutthroat deal breaker where Joan must choose between her sanity and peace, pushing her up the last step of the "Golden Ladder," or give up her personal power and stay forever one step away from the top.

(It is at this point that I became very good friends with ED. I experienced everything listed in every menopause book written, and I also created a few new ones of my own. It started simple enough—heart palpitations, minor hot flashes, memory loss and mental fogginess. Then it progressed into something more mysterious and serious. My immune system ran amuck and my weight dropped down to 94 pounds. Life was looking grim. Now of course, this just didn't happen out of the blue. I had to add just a little extra stress to the ED equation by making the decision to initiate a major landscaping remodel at the peak of my depletion. Well, viola...there you have it, all systems shut down. Now, here's the catch: even though the stress from the project was almost unbearable, I needed to stay the course. You see, to me, this was what I knew I needed to create that "cocoon" space for my emergence. It was to be my haven for my mid-life crisis. Tough? Oh yes...worth it? You betcha.)

The Backyard, Buddha, and Beer. Joan continues searching for her long lost desire and for health and wellness in the second book of this series. This story takes you on a journey of an unattended, rundown yard (and relationship) and shares the healing power of creating visual beauty while trying to maintain sanity. But not all beauty shows up wrapped in a pretty container. Suspense abounds as drama upon drama unfold during this backyard "remodel." The blessed Buddha mysteriously arrives and takes a spot in the front yard, which helps soothe pain and fosters healing. The beer? Possibly what keeps Buddha so happy!

(I can keep this one simple. My vision for a landscape remodel was waaaayyyy different than that of my beloved spouse. Not only did we disagree on design, but also the on process, development, time and financial scale. My husband, bless his heart, conceded and I chose, planned and instigated the creation for my nesting. Do you think it went as planned? Oh nooooo! We experienced an unplanned septic system overhaul, irrigation overflows and concrete pool decking popping out, just to name a few. Then one day when I was at my lowest, the UPS man delivered a package. Buddha had arrived. I sat in wonderment over the timing of this precious gift and was also baffled as to where he came from. Again, it is the thoughtfulness of friends that sometimes becomes the light that shines on your darkness. Mr. Buddha quickly found his home next to my beautiful pond under the shading Japanese Maple tree, where I see and honor him daily. It is in this spot that I came to regroup. It is this spot that not only revived my spirit and strength, but also quenched my thirst.)

The Rise and Fall of Marriage or The Day the Chair Got Kicked Out From Beneath Me. The third and final story in our trilogy, Joan finds herself sitting on the therapist's couch. Reliving all the gory details of her burned out libido, and half-completed yard. Tears of joy and sorrow abound in this comedy/drama and Joan begs her beloved to fight for what she knows to be true—that opposites do indeed attract.

(They say that if you ever want to test your relationship, do a remodel. They also should add that if, on top of this, you are exhausted and menopausal, you might as well just go ahead and start scheduling your appointments with a therapistt. It's one thing to be stressed and exhausted. It's another to be totally clueless as to the needs of your significant other. There are some things in life that, no matter how tired you are, or how pissed off you may be, you just can't neglect, unless you want to toss that in the garbage too.)

Guess Who's Coming to Dinner or, Was That an Angel That Just Flew Over? Fiction or non-fiction—you decide. Strange, paranormal incidents begin to happen to this family. Are they scared off or will they be welcomed and studied? Mystic or psychotic, that is the true question. Angels, guides and clairvoyant energy join the author as she finds her new sense of self. This is a lesson she must learn and accept with grace and gratitude in order to become who she, deep down, knows she is meant to be.

(The more intimate I became with ED, the stronger my clairvoyant self became. Even though he has taken so much away from me, he has brought me so much more in return. What I used to deem the land of "WooHoo" is now my normal day. What seemed so embarrassing and shameful now has become my most precious gift. As I've come to understand the nature of being intuitive, I've begun embracing that part of myself which is the core of who I am.)

The Great Shift. Peace at last. To become one's true self is the topic of this book. Learning and sharing all there is with those around you. Knowing that no matter what comes your way, it is only a blessing when you are able to share.

(For me, stepping into my place of power was not an easy transition. Opening up myself to the experiences of living with my intuitive gifts, and then putting them to work for the greater good has not been easy. But you know what? When you can clearly see yourself for what you are and you choose to live an honorable and loving life, things just seem to work out. It was also this "shift" that really allowed me to see this book, and the potential it had for the greater good. For that, I am ever so thankful.)

Gardening Tips

*M*y teenagers are in full bloom, in all respects. The male of the species is strong, aggressive and assertive, while the female is emotional, headstrong and empathetic. It is a garden to be maintained and cared for with great tenderness and patience. One thing that has happened is that I have begun to bloom in my midlife, just like my kids in their teens. Like many women, I'm growing emotionally, seeking to find my true path and to find a way to express my newfound strength and spiritual self. But, like my little teen garden, I'm also sprouting…zits. I too am experiencing prepubescent hell— looking in the mirror and fighting the urge to pop a zit. It is now 6:00 a.m., and I've been awake since 4:00. I've had my morning cup of toxin, which appears to not have had the effect I really need to get the day rolling. (Yes, unfortunately, I fell off the pure healthy diet wagon.) Maybe splashing some ice cold water in my face will jumpstart my system.

Splash…shiver…then tractor beam eyes straight to the big, fat whiteheads strategically located on my "chin-u-cheek" (that area that sits between the lower part of the middle aged jowl and the deep crease of the chin). As I stand, staring into the mirror, I hear myself say to my kids: "Don't pick. If you pop that, you'll regret it. It's gonna get infected and leave a big scar." Suddenly, I feel my arms raise and my hands being brought to the target zone as if I've got a magnet implanted in my face. I can't stop…its inevitable. I'm headed for the big pop.

The beauty of sitting in the same garden, tilling the same soil is that gardening techniques can be shared. That morning, the first thing brought to my attention from my daughter was: "Geez Mom, nice zit. You know if you just put toothpaste on it at night it will go away!" (She said this with the ah-duh sigh.) Toothpaste? Are you kidding me? This sounds like a ploy to sit and laugh at the dumb adult who is willing to do anything to not return to the land of puberty. Well, maybe I'll try it. Just in case.

Cool thing about toothpaste is, that not only does it whiten, brighten and refresh, it also amazingly sucks the whiteheads right out of your body. Now I wouldn't recommend doing it the way I did, which was to apply it to multiple zits, forget you have it on your face, drive the kids to school while waving and smiling to all your friends, only to come home 20 minutes later and discover you now have red, burned areas where zits once were. But I imagine if applied without an exhausted, menopausal mindset, it might just work!

Where Will You Be When the Angels Sing?

Do you believe in Angels? Spirit Guides? Universal good juju? I do. This is another thing I know for sure: we are not alone. Now some of you may be thinking that all this lack of sleep has gotten to me, that somewhere, those synapses stopped working together and now I'm imagining or hallucinating this magical energy force. Well, I hate to break it to you, but that's not true. I know that God Spirit or Universal Spirit exists. I have personally experienced it too many times to not acknowledge it any more. It is powerful, fun and transformative if you allow it into your life. I often think my ability to write is guided by some other force besides me.

I would like to challenge you. If you don't believe in The Force, take one hour out of your day and ask for an angel to guide you. Then sit quietly and pay attention to "that little voice" in your head, or that special "gut" feeling. See what happens in your day, and notice if things are different for you. Notice the subtle shifts. Who knows, this may just rock your world. Now wouldn't that be something?

If you already believe, then give your angel a big hello and hug, cuz ya know…all's good! Just my thoughts on it, that's all.

A Match Made in Heaven

*T*oday it has come to my attention that I probably am not attending to my daily tasks these last several months as well as I thought I was. My day was plugging along as usual; I had just finished my coffee, had eaten a bit of breakfast then started unloading last night's dishes from the dishwasher. Things changed for me the instant I dropped one of the spoons back into the dishwasher by accident. It was at that moment, as I reached in to grab the spoon out, I discovered much to my horror—the inside of my dishwasher. Suffice it to say, I think I could have made two more meals just with the byproducts left unseen inside this cleaning machine—macaroni bowties, spinach and something that looked like meatloaf, although I couldn't remember the last time I made meatloaf. I think if I were feeling "perky" and well rested, I may have taken the time at that moment to clean it out, but I wasn't, so I didn't. Exhaustion made it possible for me not to see it and menopause made me not give a shit, so I closed the door and pressed wash. Ew—yuck. Fortunately, I'm also a germ-a-phobe, so after the wash cycle had completed itself, I wiped out what was left and then hit wash one more time. Now I can rest in peace.

Battle of the Sexes…

*S*o today, while in the shower, I have this random thought. Marriage is like living in a parallel universe with someone. Every day you are living side by side, eating, playing and resting together, most times feeling the symbiotic flow of companionship that marriage brings. Well, that is until conversation comes into play. It is at that moment for my husband and I, that we get teleported back to our own individual universes. My dear hubby and I can sit in the same room, talk about the same thing, each thinking that we are speaking each other's language, only to find out that we have no clue what the other just said or meant. Now I know that this isn't a new and novel idea, but it really is fascinating to me. What kind of a twisted "maker" do we have? I can just imagine the conversation that God had:

"I think I'll have half of the species speak, and at the same time the other half will convert that information to something close, but not totally accurate. That way they will communicate in circles…like watching a cat chase its tail. Round and round they'll go…but never really getting anywhere. Silly little humans."

Finances are a big communicating block for us. I live by the refrigerator magnet motto—"How can I be overdrawn? I still have checks." My husband lives by (I'll admit it here and now, a much smarter philosophy), "Work hard, save money and pay cash." Booooorrrrrrrring… Miss Leo the lion says, "Beauty surrounds me. Creativity abounds me." Mr. Cancer the crab says, "I'm comfortable here in my little hut, my protective shell. I need no rearranging, decorating. I'm content in my shell." Miss Leo says, "Trinkets, gadgets, new technology!" Mr. Cancer says, "No excess stuff and wasteful mechanics." Miss Leo says, "It's clearly broken, buy a new and better one!" Mr. Cancer says, "There's nothing wrong with this one. I'll just fix it and it will be like new."

Now after all these years of marriage (over four of those with me being a sleep-deprived, hormonally starved, maniac), we have finally figured out a system of communication that works for us. Once Leo the lion starts to roar (that would be me), Cancer the crab holds up his claw to signal a break (that would be him). Off to our own respective corners we go. Once it has cooled down enough to where Miss. Leo no longer has the desire to eat Mr. Crab in one bite, we come back together to chat. Honestly, we agree to disagree about 50% of time. The other 50%

you will just have to use your imagination to guess how the battle goes. I will just say this: If you put a lion and a crab in a boxing ring, the end result just isn't pretty, no matter how you look at it.

Nobody "Nose" the Trouble I've Smelled

My sense of smell has gotten me into trouble many times over. You see, I am a "scenta-holic." I constantly smell things, real and imagined. Most of our marital disputes the last several years have been based on me and my nose. Upon my insistence, we fixed propane "leaks" that we never could find (to the extent of replumbing the house), and we ripped walls apart looking for the dead mouse that never appeared. I have forced my husband underneath the house (a less than two-foot crawl space) to hunt for mold and other toxic, aromatic fungi, only to be told that all is well. I have tossed out lunchmeat as it is being laid on slices of bread and have dumped delicious beverages down the drain all because, "it smells funny."

The last several days it all began again, this time in the garage. I knew we had a mouse trapped somewhere, probably a little gift from our big, fat cat Kramer. In passing, I mention to my beloved, "Ew, it stinks in here. I think there's a dead mouse." Now usually this prompts him to get a move on and start searching for the little bugger, but not this time. Something had changed in my man. That day I got a look and a shrug. Oh my God, he's become immune! I have no more leverage…I've lost the edge. This left me pondering, "How am I going to get this dead critter out of here?" So, like any smart lady, I did nothing. I figured if I waited long enough, the stink would become so bad that he'd have to notice and then would just take care of it. Several days went by, each getting stinkier and stinkier, so bad as a matter of fact that the smell was now permeating into the house through the exterior wall. "Can't you smell that? Oh this is getting gross. I'm going to go out and move the freezer and see what I can find." So, at 9:30 p.m. on a Saturday night, out to the garage I went, proudly wearing my "brave" hat. All I can say is thank God I was eventually followed by my Hero—Captain Mouse Remover! Praise the Lord!

I have to admit the look on his face was less than enthusiastic, but we began moving and shifting cabinets out of the way in order to locate our newest guest at the Bates Motel. "All hands on deck! All hands on deck! We have a big one!" "Did you find something?" I daintily asked. "You may want to go inside," the Captain announced. "It's big, possibly a possum or cat." That's all it took. Off went my gloves, down went my broom, and into the house I scurried.

I have no problem admitting when I'm out of my league, and folks…the night of the decaying bunny, did me in. I went to bed that night seriously contemplating whether or not country living was really worth it after all.

Please Oh Please! Just a Little Peace and Quiet!!

*M*outh noises freak me out. I'm not sure what happened to me in a past life but I can't stand the sounds of chewing, chomping, grinding and swallowing. If you need me to exit a room quickly, just start chewing with gusto and my little patootie will be out the door in two seconds flat. You can also use this as a form of torture to get me to quickly tell you anything you need me to say. Just take me for a little "car ride," then start chewing. Better yet, get a good rhythm going, something like: "Hand in bag of nuts—crinkle, crinkle, crinkle—Nut in mouth—chew chew chew—Hand in bag of nuts—crinkle, crinkle, crinkle—Nut in mouth—chew chew chew—Hand in bag of nuts—crinkle, crinkle, crinkle—Nut in mouth—chew chew chew. Repeat over and over for miles of endless miles. You want to know my PIN number? You got it. My age? No problem. Weight? All yours. Just please, stop with the mouth noises.

Tonight I sit in the living room, hiding from the tortilla chip crunch and the blasting TV. I have closed doors and turned up the stereo just to drown out the noise. But, like in so many areas of my life, I'm discovering that the universe really has a very twisted sense of humor, I suppose one very similar to mine. Just as I start to enjoy this sanctuary of peace and quiet, in trots the dog, our sweet, faithful old Labrador Retriever, with her hard, labored breathing and stiff joints, grumbling like a little old lady with the worst case of "cotton mouth" I've ever heard. So tonight, instead of screaming and running out of the room, I choose to embrace the moment, enjoy the music and smile at the wonderful memories this "sweet old gal" has given me. Drool, slobber and hugs and kisses to my Miss Kate.

The Day I Took the Leaf Blower to the Dog

Where oh where is she going with this story you ask? Well, unfortunately for me and fortunately for you, this is the day that I am going to bare one of my deepest, darkest secrets…I lied to my vet. You see, my Miss Kate not only has really bad "cotton mouth," but nasty, nasty skin too. For months, we have been working to get her to keep her fur to herself, and not deposit it all over our house. Hundreds of dollars in medications, foods and medicated shampoos have now brought us to this point in history.

The last several weeks have been a challenge. Trying to shove four, huge pills down a dog's throat while she is on an "elimination" diet, has taken its toll on me. A sleepless dog owner with tendonitis, and a crafty dog that spits the pills back out when you aren't looking, is a bad mix. Now, on top of the pill-o-rama, we are to be enjoying a "therapeutic" bath, one per week as a matter of fact. Would it be a big surprise if I told you that the baths didn't happen either? Probably not.

So, on this beautiful Friday morning, I stumble to the calendar to see what I have on my schedule for today. Shit, a recheck at the vet for the dog. I find it so interesting that I now start to experience a familiar sense of panic, almost as bad as if I had just robbed the local bank. What I think the vet may do to me, I'm not sure, but I clearly sense that I don't even want to begin to imagine. I frantically look at the clock and realize that I have 30 minutes before I have to be there. I slam down the rest of my coffee, inhale the remaining tidbits of oatmeal in my bowl and run out the door.

Katie doesn't have a spa where she is bathed. She has to be on display in the front yard where she clearly lets me know that she is horrified to be out in public in this less-than-desirable condition. Head hung low, ears drooping, tail tucked between her legs and the most pitiful gaze in her big, brown eyes, "How could you!?" she pleads. Hose on, dog wet, shampoo applied, dog rinsed…then I remember; you don't quickly *dry* a Labrador Retriever. It's almost impossible. When God made these guys, I think he started with a layer of sponge. I have no idea where all the water goes, and where it all keeps coming from.

Remember, it's about 8:15 in the morning and I clearly am not at my best. I quickly start to gather as many towels as possible. (It is now that I wish I had my super absorbent "Sham-Wow" cloth.) Five towels later and she is still dripping from places that I swear I've wiped. What the heck?! I run into the house and grab the blow dryer. Katie by now has given up. She has lain down, rolled over and is trying to hide her head under the car. It is quite a pathetic scene. Sweat dripping from my brow. I turn my head to wipe my forehead and then I see it—the LEAF BLOWER. It's the first time I've ever noticed the golden, heavenly glow emanating from it. Just think of the blowing power! Wham-Bam we'd be done soooo quick!

Katie meets my gaze, and then looks out the corners of her eyes to the blower, then back at me. "You've got to be kidding me, Mom," she says. Thank God she speaks English, because after that brief interaction, I came to my senses. More towels, more hair drying and a few minutes late to our appointment, but no leaf blower.

Katie and I got a good report from our vet. She felt the baths (plural) were really working and chose to lighten the burden on me and give Katie a shot, verses having us continue with the pill dance. I'm thrilled. Katie…not so much.

Dearly Departed

I realized this morning that I never mentioned how "Larry" passed away. Larry was one of the unfortunate victims of a "smell-o-holic" rampage during the time when I was ill. It was a crisp, winter morning and the beautiful, California sky was ocean-blue. It was a day just made for deep cleaning the house. Since dust and country living go hand and hand, I knew reinforcements were going to be necessary. I thought I had a good plan. We would do surface wiping, curtain cleaning, and valance vacuuming, as well as sucking up all the mystery items from underneath the furniture that hadn't been moved for years. What I didn't anticipate was a clever cleaning lady and a deadly bottle of Windex. Did you know if you spray Windex on furniture, (yea, Windex on furniture…go figure) you can create an "off gassing" from the ammonia in the Windex and the leather conditioner on the sofa? Take it from me, you can.

As you can imagine, my nose went crazy and my rundown immune system sent up red flags. "Get out!

Get out! Danger, danger!" I would compare this feeling to living in a gas chamber, however I have no idea what that really would be like. I'm sure you can guess what happened next. Larry was moved to the garage and covered with plastic to protect him from the invasion of mice, and to protect me from him. Now if I were thinking clearly then, I would have realized that if there was a strong enough toxic odor coming from Larry, I would have found dead mice all around him before *I* would have dropped to the ground, but of course I didn't. I can tell you this; Larry was not invited back in. He had been blacklisted and removed.

Here's the part that I just feel bad about. After several weeks we "passed" Larry on to another family. I struggled with this decision. How could I refuse to poison my family, yet expose my friends to this flow of toxic fumes? I'll tell you how: they're not crazy like me. I'm happy to report that Larry is being loved and adored by a wonderful family (who, by the way, are all still alive and well). I believe he is even being allowed to be himself, just a plain old comfy couch instead of a support system for a sleepless crab.

Oh What a Bitch

The reason I thought of Larry this morning was because I spent last night on "Lillithe," our new couch. She is something else! Sleek, angular, semi-padded but not overstuffed. Firm…yes, *very* firm. I'm not sure she and I will become true friends. While I really enjoy her daytime demeanor, she is quite a bitch at night. I woke up stiff and less flexible than I was when I went to bed, so I can only imagine what would become of me if I spend too much time in her presence. Not a pretty sight.

I've begun to have some terrific fantasies about places to acquire sleep. One of them involves a local hotel and maid service. Oh my, how wonderful.

I'm Pretty Ass-Backwards

As I stand in my creative thinking box (the shower), I become aware that I must be getting comfortable and relaxed in my life. I've come to this conclusion because I notice that my feet are quickly disappearing. In just a few short months, my body has improved from a depleted and rundown 94-pound weakling, to a healthy, round, 120-pound beauty. Praise the Lord! Curse the clothes. This topic comes up today because I am preparing to venture out into the land of "Shopping." I hate it there. You see, I've waited until the very last minute to get a dress for a wedding, so I can no longer avoid this trip. Now my idea of Shopping is standing in a changing room with a glass of "sparkly" while someone hands me things to put on, but of course that isn't my reality. So today I take the high road and head to the mall.

Mile after mile I walk, looking for that perfect place to stop and rest, a place to rejuvenate my attire by finding a new dress, and as usual, I end up in the very first store where I was sure nothing would work. I drape four dresses over my arm and grumble as I stomp off into the changing room. I immediately fall in love with this sleek little number—pinks, purples and greens all flowing to the ground like a soft, angelic uniform. I know I would never be able to earn anything angelic in this lifetime or any other lifetime, which is why I'm so drawn to it. I stand in front of the mirror twirling and swaying, fondling the "fabric" not the "material." (Just ask my friend Kim. She's a real stickler for the designer vocab.) A quick note on Kim: she is the only woman I know who can get a group of men to understand the difference between "fabric" and "material." You *wear* fabric. You make a *car* out of material—very different. And don't get them mixed up when she's around. That's just not tolerated.

Anyway, back to this angelic, flowing dress and the others that didn't make the cut. (That's actually going to be a funny pun later in this story.) This one was definitely worthy of a second try on after all the others were tossed in a pile on the dressing room floor. Yes, it was beautiful yet simple, elegant but not gaudy. Something, however, didn't look right. Something was definitely wrong. Then I figured it out. It appeared that I was wearing it backwards. The big ole fat seam straight up the front of the dress should have been an immediate clue, but when shopping in a sleepless daze, some things do go unnoticed. So, with my daughter laughing hysterically at me and my fopaux, I turn the dress around. Uh oh, still not right. My boobs have now taken a turn for the worse and have either shrunk or voluntarily relocated to my back. The dress is hanging on the top, yet flowing "seamlessly" down the front. What the hell!? Back the other way…nope…turn around again…nope.

Believe it or not, I bought the dress anyway. After all, it was on sale. If I can't figure out how to open the seam up and turn it around, then I guess I'll just have to wear it ass-backwards…literally. In reality, that won't be much different than how I function day to day with little sleep. Ass-backwards… but at least I'll be pretty!

Yin vs. Yang

I think the universe wants me to look at dualities…yin vs. yang, big vs. little, hard vs. soft, black vs. white, but mostly man vs. animal. It began two days ago. They came to enlighten and to send me messages from beyond.

Have you ever almost stepped on a snake? Nothing gets your attention quicker than a big blob of black and white snake. OK, maybe one with a rattle on the end would perk you up a little bit more, but for me, this was plenty! Now, when discussing snakes, my natural tendency is to set the bias that it is a big bad "He" snake, never a soft, loving "She" snake. So for the direct purpose of painting the portrait of a villain, my snake is now deemed a "HE."

At 9:30 p.m., with my arms full of laundry, I venture into the house from the garage where my washer and dryer are. With sheets piled high in my arms, I have about ¼ inch of viewing space accessible to me. After 15 years of country living, I have successfully conquered the art of tree frog dodging to get in the house. It's kind of like doing the hoedown: "Swing your partner round and round, watch those froggies on the ground." Gross, but true. But never, ever have I had to: "Swing your partner round and round, don't wet your pants there's a snake on the ground!"

As you can imagine, I looked at Him, and screamed my lungs out while jumping a good four feet in the air. He looked at me, wet his pants and slithered into the bushes directly outside my door! The thing that really angered me was that no one else in the family saw the travesty or the urgency of this situation. My husband managed to get up, grab a stick, make a few small jabs in the bushes and then declared there was nothing more he could do. Personally, I think there was a lot more he could do. He could get my pruning sheers, clip all the bushed back, catch the snake and relocate it in my neighbor's field. That would be good for starters.

That night I went to bed with the "Heebie Jeebies," just waiting for "Him" to slither into my house and crawl into bed with me. Instead, what I got was another visitor, different, yet just as annoying. After dozing off into slumber land, I was gently wakened by the smell of fresh, percolating coffee. As I yawned and stretched, I wondered why my alarm hadn't gone off. Huh, 3:30 a.m. Why am I making coffee at 3:30 in the morning? Then I wake up. It is *not* coffee…but rather a skunk. Here we go again with the black and white theme. So out of bed I climb, flashlight in hand (just in case that snake has made its way in), to close all the windows in the house.

That's country living for you. By the next day I had calmed down and decided to try and block out of my memory the two "S's." Like most things in my life though, I never just have "an" incident; there are usually multiple incidents and this occasion of course was no different. No more slithering or stinking—just a little mouse, that ran over my foot and into the chair. That sealed the deal. $S^2 + M$ does not $=$peace and serenity. It just made me cry. The End.

The Confessions of a Housewife Drug Dealer

*A*gain, I feel the need to confess another deep, dark secret. I drugged my husband. Now mind you, I didn't do it intentionally, but I drugged him just the same. I didn't even realize it until it was too late (about 11:30 p.m. on Sunday night). Just to clarify, the drug I'm speaking of was caffeine.

Here's how my confession goes: Dear Lord, please forgive my transgressions. You see, all I really wanted was an indoor laundry room. Nothing too terribly fancy, just a little something where I'm not picking dehydrated frogs out of my laundry soapbox. I only meant to provide my man slave with a cool, liquid refreshment after his many long hours of work. OK, so it did occur to me as I was pouring the 16 oz glass of thick, black liquid, that I may have steeped the tea bags a little too long, or that the third tablespoon of lemonade mix that I added probably contained just as much sugar as one would consume eating a box of Hostess Ding-Dongs, but honestly, I just wanted to do something nice for him in return.

I should have realized after several attempts at trying to get him to take a break for dinner, that something was not right. I should have seen the signs, but I didn't. I could only see that see he was on a mission, and I was happy. It was only as the sky was getting darker that I saw the first indications of the overdose. I will never forget the glazed, dazed look in his eyes, the grinding sound of his teeth and the speed of the words spewing from his mouth, "It's 8:30 p.m. already? Geez it's late. I guess I could take a break, but maybe I'll just finish this last spot. Can you move the extra tools over there? How about helping me with clean up? Oh can you hand me that trowel?" All the while, he was continuing to slather goo on the walls. But you see, I still needed drywall, I still needed tape and texture, I needed completion, so I allowed it to continue without interruption. You see, after surviving my little country hoedown with wildlife, just days before, I had to have this project done.

My poor man slave didn't sleep well that night. After hours of hard, manual labor he should have dropped right off to sleep, but instead he was up channel surfing, just like his sleep-deprived wife. It was then that I realized what I had done and I truly felt bad. But the evil forces that make me want to conquer my environment and become ruler of my home are strong...I am determined to win this battle of man vs. animal on the farm. And if I can't be supreme ruler, then at least maybe I can become Queen of my Soap Box once again.

Father, please forgive my sins.

I'm Not King of the Underworld...I'm Not, I'm Not, I'm Not!

This book began because I lacked sleep. I still do. Since I began writing, I have had only brief moments of truly feeling rested. I was hoping that I would have some epiphany for how to become rested while staying connected in real life, but I just don't see that as an option. I thought maybe I would stumble upon a special technique or potion to gently rock us sleep-deprived people into the land of the unconscious. I don't see that happening either. What concerns me the most is that I really don't see an end to this, if I want my life to continue as it is, in all other respects.

Why wouldn't I change things if it meant getting sleep? Well, I don't think my spouse would be thrilled to be kicked to the curb (or a least to another bed), for one. I think I would be faced with a major protest that would drain me more than not sleeping.

Last night I dreamed of a bat that turned into a baby. Maybe my ticket is to sleep all day like a bat; then I will become rested and playful like a brand new baby. Or maybe I'm just a freak who is so exhausted that she can't even have normal dreams. While there are several different meanings in dream interpretation of the bat (one involving King of the Underworld), I doubt that I am destined for evil. More than likely it is my subconscious screaming, "God girl, you're an evil, wicked bitch without sleep!" As with the yin/yang in everything in life, so is there the yin/yang in dream interpretation. The other bat meaning is that of rebirth, newness, intuitiveness and understanding things at their most basic, psychic nature. Now that rings true for me. And if I add the baby into the mix…well, that's just the proper combination for success.

So, as I leave this train of thought, this is what I take with me: no magical cure for the sleep-deprived, not the King of the Underworld. Unfortunately though, probably the evil bitch. I will hope for a renewal…if not in rest of the physical body, then of the spirit. Maybe today I will just sleep in the sun.

My Core Weakness is Now Exposed

I've been rolling this idea around in my head for the last several days, so it must have some meaning or purpose of thought. I'm not sure how it will begin, transform or end, but I think it is supposed to be put into the written word, so here it goes.

I wonder what makes the human spirit continue to do things that it knows are detrimental to the physical body.

Like I stated before (or at least I think I stated before…maybe it was in another book…who knows, I'm too tired to care), I have tons of addictions— things I do over and over and over without really caring about the end result because I get a high from them. In the end I feel like crap, but just the thought of that rush is soooooo worth all the pain that comes afterward. No, I'm not talking about sniffing glue in the family room, and heaven forbid I'm not doing liners on the bathroom mirror. It's chocolate that gets me.

*A note on addiction: I am by no means making fun of anyone with a serious addiction, because what I know for sure is that regardless of the substance or action, the end result is the same. There is a lack of control with a detrimental outcome that hinders healthy living. I honor and respect those who are living with addictions and my intention is only to shed light on my own process.

OK, now back to chocolate. I have had an on-again, off-again relationship with this drug, and I truly believe it's a drug, when you start ingesting the quantities that I'm talking about. I'm squirting it in my coffee, rolling it in my mouth, pinching off pieces and popping rollie pollies. It is in powdered form, solid form, ooey gooey liquid form. I just saw a body cream that could allow me to smear it all over my body if I wanted to. Now that would be pure heaven. I have Kisses in my living room and office, truffles in the kitchen and chocolate mints in my purse. I'm telling you, it's bad.

For me, it's not about the end result of layers of padding on my butt. No, this action will actually make me quite physically ill, yet I continue to do it because I feel I need the high to get me going or keep me moving. Here's the kicker: after I'm physically ill, I can't do anything anyway because I'm sick. It's like giving yourself the flu, over and over again.

I know there is the chemical component to addiction, but there is also a spiritual component and I suspect it plays a significant role too. Why would "I" allow this vessel that "I" live in to become rundown and sick on purpose, over and over again? I'll tell you why, because that stuff is gooooood, oh so goooooood. It's smooth, soft, rich and sweet. It smells warm and loving. It is an acceptable adult pacifier.

So this morning I've primped, prepped, poured chocolate in my coffee and pondered why I continue to do this—especially since I'm feeling sick. I'm looking for my Oprah ah-ha moment. Where are you Miss Oprah? The only thing I come up with is that it has to do with anger and punishment. After all, it's easier to beat yourself up instead of someone else. I guess the next piece of the puzzle is what am I angry about? Maybe because I'm dreaming that I'm King of the Underworld and I know that's just not true, or maybe it's because I feel so shortchanged that others get to sleep and I don't. But maybe it's simply because chocolate is so damn good and I'm angry that God didn't make it one of our "we need it to survive" phytonutrients. Yeah, that's it, mystery solved.

Oh Lord, Please No More!

*L*ast night I was awakened three times—two times from nightmares, and one time by Kramer the cat. In the short time span from 1:30 a.m. to 4:00 a.m., I tried to: put out a fire in my barn in order to save some chickens (which I do not have), put on tennis shoes so that when I put the fire out my feet would be covered, called 911 and opened the door to greet the three firemen who told me that the chickens didn't survive. Then I went to my friend's office to get a house key for the address of 621, followed my friend down a hallway to see an old woman convalescing (I think I've met her before), continued to follow her to a long set of stairs, which I climbed to get my dogs. After seeing my three dogs I realized there was a very bad man chasing me and I fell down. At that moment he chose to tower over me with the intention of doing me great harm. I screamed and kicked him so hard that he crumbled and evaporated.

Wonder woman? Or…boy, I wonder about you woman! Or…boy, it's no wonder you don't feel rested, woman. You decide. As for Kramer the cat, I guess I will have to be responsible for letting him out at night as apparently I can't trust my teenager to remember.

Could You Please Stop the Ride?
I Would Like to Get Off Now

The energy in my house is bizarre. I have two angry teenagers blasting music and slamming doors, the dog is freaking out because the "bug" man is here to spray, toilets are plugging up while the washing machine clunks along. I have had endless interruptions of all types, but still I feel the need to get this on paper. I guess one important note to make is that when Spirit speaks, you just follow. No matter what.

I'm 47 years old and too tired to wash my face at night. I have been keenly aware of my lack of control and my lack of desire to be in control of my body's health. I can't continue this. I have to be done with this phase in my life. What is making this dysfunctional cycle continue? What is in my dark side that allows this self-abuse to continue? Why must I always give in to and resort back to the negative habits, just as the positive changes begin to make me stronger? Well, no more. I just can't afford it anymore. Sugar is pain to my body, caffeine is pain to my body, lack of sleep is pain to my body and my psyche. Pain meds shorten the physical pain but prolong the psyche's pain and exacerbate the pain from lack of control. It is small in the grand scheme of things, but grand in the smallness of my organic, physical self.

I honor my strength that has gotten me through so many painful situations. I honor my backbone, stamina and sense of humor. I need to see this as my one and only chance to change. I can't continue to be so casual about it. Today I have been grumpy…well, actually just bitchy. I have not felt honored in any way, shape or form. I have not felt respected, and while I feel basic, motherly love from my kids, I just don't feel special.
I'm angry at me. I'm angry for holding on to secrets…mine of course. I'm angry that this is one of the life lessons I've chosen to learn so that I can transform myself to a higher state of being. Now that that's said, I am also so grateful for this journey that I am about to embark on. I envision it to be easy, smooth, magical, fantastic and of course, transformative. From this moment forward I look toward the light for strength and guidance. And when I feel weakness and pain coming on, I will step through it, for it is what I need to do. I am not alone, and I am not, by far, in one of the deepest spots that one could be in. I am blessed, for from this journey, I will step into me, my wholeness, my shining moment—me, the shining star. The breath of light shall save me. The breath of light shall guide and

support me. The breath of light will take me to the places of health, wealth and harmony where I long to be. And when breath can't take me there, the pen will be my friend, my guide, my soul for my journey.

I long to "remove" myself from the mundane, everyday life in order to heal my soul, but I think it may be the mundane that just will save my soul. Day dreams of spa treatments, quiet fluffy beds and warm rays of sun offer healing that I need, but in fact all I need is me, quiet contemplation, good food, love and grace.

I remain open to the healing my guides bring for me. In Gratitude.

One of the things I've noticed is that, yes, I'm even too tired to prepare a simple, healthy lunch. My body craves the pure, clean goodness of the simple foods, yet the very thought of preparing it makes me want to drop to my knees and cry. Why oh why can't someone just cook for me until I become strong and rested? I noticed this, noted it and then began the arduous task of slicing zucchini to be steamed.

It was quick and simple and actually quite painless. Why did the thought of this bring such turmoil into my life? Why would the thought of this simple task normally just send me to the refrigerator for cheese, chips and an ice cold beer? I can tell that my body is too acidic; my joints are stiff, painful and popping more than a bag of Jiffy Pop. But even knowing that, I normally would just slink to the fridge, toss stuff onto a paper plate, pop a cold one and then sit. But not today. Today I will ponder all of these actions, but in the long run, re-act with the intention to heal. Each step will be with thoughtfulness, strength and praise. I am woman. Hear Me Roar!

Sugar Whore

"OH YOO HOO, I'm in here!" Mr. Vanilla Vanilla yelled. "You know you want me baby. You know you need me. Just sashay over here and give me a little lick."

Nothing is worse than nighttime "Boredom Porn" from the freezer. You know it's there and you know you want it. You know it will temporarily take you to a place of ecstasy that will shake you to your inner core, yet you know it can also be the downfall of all that is good and healthy. I struggle with this as I harbor 1.5 quarts of Dryers Double Vanilla in my freezer.

I didn't bring it into the house; my family did, in honor of my birthday. I find it kind of funny that we will celebrate our lives with sugary treats that in the long run will ultimately be our demise. What a great celebratory tradition. "Glad you made it to 47 years pal, let's load your body and vessels up with cholesterol and spike your insulin to see how long you can really last!" Cruel, really cruel.

I did indulge on my birthday, a huge scoop of ice cream topped with whipping cream, just in case the first load didn't work. I did, however, pile fresh blackberries on top for their "anti-oxidant" properties—you know, being of health-minded consciousness and all. I love living in the moment. I love being of mind, body and spirit, for when my mind says, "Dude, just have a bite," my body will be the first to scream, "Yeah, dude, do it, just do it!" as my spirit dances in exaltation knowing that the other two are weak and stupid because it knows—"Hallelujah, heaven it on its way!"

No European Spa Here!

This past week I decided I needed to go on a Spiritual/Healing Retreat, so I cleared my calendar in preparation for this monumental event. The timing seemed right. I was feeling run down, had pain in every joint of my body and was looking for some Divine Intervention to heal my body and soul. I decided to check out of my life and venture into the land of introspection in the hopes of finding some well-needed answers.

I can now see some flaws in the logic of trying this from home in the middle of summer, but as I've stated before, I'm stubborn and usually have to do things my way. I suppose I should have reconsidered as the week progressed, maybe even postponed it until the conditions were more agreeable, but I figured part of this journey was to have some stamina in order to be successful, so I endured.

First, I'll share with you what I had envisioned this event would be like and what I believed I would have achieved after a weeklong retreat. Each day would begin with waking up on my own. No alarm clocks would be welcome here at "Chateau de la R & R." I would start each day with a cup of tea (not my normal cup of coffee) and then gently slip into some newfound Yoga poses. I would lovingly chant my new mantra, *"All is well. Peace and healing come my way with ease and grace,"* as each new day began. Breakfast would be of healthy contents—only organic meats, fruits and vegetables would be allowed. Mid morning would include reading, writing and walking. Naps in the sun by the pool were a must. Reading, writing, sleeping—yes, that was the planned theme for the week. I would continue to nourish my body and spirit this way for five, glorious days. By Friday I would feel elated. I would have increased flexibility, my skin would have an extra glow, and the bags under my eyes would have magically disappeared. I no longer would crave the sugar crap that keeps me running. I would have clear thought and smooth flowing energy. I would emerge renewed.

Do you think just once things would go my way? Just once the great Universal Powers would say, "Ya know, she's really trying to get her act together. Let's give her what she thinks she needs, just once and see what happens." Noooooooo, of course not! That would be too simple.

I never saw the sun that week because we were fogged in…in August. My stiff and painful joints only got worse and I did anything I could to keep my body warm, including drinking coffee. I did add more veggies to my diet, but found my hand in the chip bag several times, mostly out of boredom and frustration at not being able to get outside. Every time I attempted a walk, the vineyard management company magically appeared with their crew to check vines or watering systems. No serenity there. I did, however, have a moment where I gained a little introspection and this is what I came up with:

My home is a place of comfort, a place where laughter at everyday circumstances gets us through the difficult times, a place where nurturing the soul comes not from profound spiritual awakenings, but from the smiles of those who live within the walls. It's about the compassionate family pet who knows when to follow and when to leave, and the friend who just magically calls to "check in." While my physical being remains in a state of upheaval, my soul dances for it knows deep down that, "this too shall pass."

Just Open Your Eyes and Pay Attention!
(If You Can)

SYMBOLISM. Yeah, symbolism. I'm not sure how I will explain to you the impact it has had on my life. I will start by telling you how every time I make a symbolic connection to something in my life and I attempt to explain it to my kids, they both roll their eyes all the way back in their heads until you can only see the whites. (How *do* they do that?) Of course this is frustrating because symbolism is something I really do want them to understand, but boy I'm at a loss.

There are so many things that happen in our day-to-day lives that we just overlook, small gifts from the universe that will have such a huge impact on our existence if we just slow down and pay attention—the tiny bird that lands right in front of us on the road, the wild animal that we have never laid eyes on near where we live, just happens to cross our path, the shimmering rock that for some reason catches our eye as we walk, or the beautiful feather we find lying all by itself on the ground. All of these simple things are of meaning, if we allow them into our lives.

Now, sometimes all of this can get a little out of hand, and I'll readily admit, I've allowed it to at times. For example, there was that day the poor bird flew directly into my kitchen window. Never mind the fact that the sun was so bright it blinded the poor little bugger as it flew into the reflection, or that I had plants inside on the windowsill that I think he was aiming for. I was sure I was destined to break my neck that day, an event that, thankfully, did not come to fruition. My teenagers think that if symbolism actually works, then there must be a reason why the package of chocolate doughnuts just magically appeared into the shopping cart...*NOT*!

There have been those times when I've allowed the message to come to me and it has, more than once, made a huge shift in my life. No, this isn't driven by my sleep deprivation. I swear—this is real. There was a point in time when I was quite ill and I didn't have any answers for what was happening to me. After a moment of quiet reflection, I asked for guidance. I'm impatient, so when I didn't get my quick, internal response, I stomped off like a pouting little child to water my garden. As I held the garden hose, an amazing thing happened; a beautiful hummingbird came for a drink. Now, normally I could justify that...come on, after all it *is* water. But this little bird took its drink, then flew up and stopped right in front of my face, giving me direct eye contact…then went down for another drink…then back in my face. This happened four times. He hovered for another moment, then left.

Sometimes I'm not that "quick," so I just thought, "that was cool," and continued pouting about the answer I never received from my meditation request. Then it hit. Water. There was this connection to my health issue and water. And you know what? It was true.

One of my many addictions is my love for books, so my sources for interpreting different symbolic messages is quite versed, but when all else fails, I go to Google. Just type in "Symbolic meaning of…" It can be quite a fun game. I have my own beliefs and theories of where these "gifts" come from. Maybe after you play the game, you'll come up with your own. Go ahead, try it…you just never know.

The Foibles of a Fatigued Farmer

Growing up I was blessed to have been raised with, and given the duty of caring for, a wide variety of animals. We always had multiple pets in or around the house. Some were gifts and some were purchased, while others came our way as the result of the bartering system for my fathers' doctoring services. I thought my mother would freak out the day he came home with a "Great Dane" in exchange for payment of a past due medical bill. There were those animals we cared for while their owners took vacations. Some of these critters never returned to their original homes, but stayed with us because the "babysitting" home was so nice. And finally, some of them just chose us. The neighbors' dogs would come by for my mother's famous peanut butter and jelly sandwiches (later to be upgraded to the ham and cheese sandwiches for their faithful patronage). Stray cats would come for their daily bowl of milk, a bowl that some family member had lovingly placed out on the back porch, and then just kept refilling, because the cats just kept showing up. There were dogs, cats, birds, guinea pigs, rats, hamsters, fish, chickens, pigs, turtles and I'm sure others that I've forgotten. In retrospect my parents were like Mr. & Mrs. Saint Francis of Assisi. I don't recall them ever turning away an animal.

It should be of no surprise then, that I too would grow up and naturally desire to surround myself with pets. When we decided to move to the country, I was so excited by the possibility of raising farm animals. We had visualized where we would raise our children, teaching them all of the intricacies of farming. Fantasies of autumn harvests and self-sustained meals ran through my head. Well…that didn't last long.

In the beginning of country living, life was simple—two dogs, one cat and one little baby. I relished in a few successful canning experiences, a flourishing garden and then the gift of a second child. I was feeling the power. I knew in my heart of hearts that I was meant to be a farming mama. Then I woke up.

Lottie the Little Rat. Our pet adventures started with Lottie, our family rat. Only six short weeks after we acquired her, we found out that she was in the motherly way. Everyone was so excited that we would soon have a nice family of rats (OK, not everyone). This was my first Fatigued Farm experience, and one I'm a little embarrassed to tell.

Lottie decided to have her babies at 3:00 a.m., not an optimal time for midwifery. It was the odd screeching sound weaving its way into my dreams, which woke me up. I had heard it before…oh yes, just like the screams that had come from me, a short five years before. They were the cries of a mother in labor. As I stumbled into my son's room with flashlight in hand to witness the miracle of birth, I quickly saw that something was very wrong.

First, I had never actually seen a "baby rat" before. One look and I definitely became weak-kneed and squeamish. God certainly did not decide to bless baby rats with being cute, that's for sure. They looked more like little worms with big eyes—not at all what I had expected. It then came to my attention that the babies were so little that they were actually falling through the wire at the bottom of the cage. Lottie had strategically placed her bottom over the biggest gap in the cage.

Now somewhere in the deep recesses of my sleepy brain, I remembered that if an animal smells a human scent on its offspring, it will usually abandon it. Thinking quickly, I ran to the kitchen to grab the biggest serving spoon that I had, in order to scoop the little worm rats back up to safety. It took a total of two hours, first to scoop, then to hold, as this poor mama rat birthed the last four, one by one out onto the spoon. Never in my wildest dreams (and boy, did I wish that it was a dream) would have thought I'd be the labor coach for our pet rat. Phew, what a job!

Feeling just a little creeped out, somewhat queasy and of course tired, I made my way to the coffee pot. 5:00 a.m.—the bewitching hour. My day had begun.

C

Hamlet and Bacon. This little piggy went to market. This little piggy did not get to stay home. As I stated before, when sleep deprivation peaks, the well-rested have very persuasive powers over the deprived, so the day my daughter asked if she could raise swine for market, my answer was a bumbling, "Well of course dear." Oh my, how cute those little piggies were—spooning each other as they snuggled in for the night. Day after day they grew more plump and powerful, all the while remaining gentle and loving. Then they got smart. It was as if overnight they decided that they had had enough, and no longer would remain penned in. The battle began between my brilliant engineer husband and the pork. It was tricky to say the least. The latch had to open easy enough for my 10-year-old daughter to maneuver, but had to be strong enough to keep the powerful pork chops in. The day the "final latch design" manifested, was the day I had had enough!

It was a chilly evening in April after a wonderful spring rain. The field grass was just starting to push its thin head up through the moist, adobe soil—green and smooth, yet not quite lush. I was finishing a therapeutic treatment with a client when I heard the noise. It was a "snort and harrumph" that I intuitively translated to, "Ya-hoo we're free!" Before I even had the opportunity to peak through the curtain, I knew what I would find: two big, fat pigs ripping up and down the field. 420 pounds of pork running at about 20 miles per hour is quite a frightening sight to say the least.

After quickly making my apologies to my client, I ran out into the muddy field in my white, working clothes to catch me up some pigs. (Actually, I was running, crying and trying to dial my cell phone all at once.) "You need to get home now and fix this damn latch! The pigs are heading for the pool!" I screamed into the phone at my husband. There I stood in the middle of my yard, wiping the tears from my exhausted eyes, waiting to be run over, as the pigs ran circles around me.

Luckily, after a couple of laps, the pigs decided food was more important than more running, and promptly followed the bucket I was holding back to the barn. By then, my husband had returned and a thick bolt lock was quickly added to their escape hatch. I was muddy, cold and tired, but at least I had won…Thaaat'sss Alllll Folkkkks.

𝓒

Here Chickie Chickie. There are actually two types of chickens—those you eat and those who are cute and become family pets. We have experienced both but unfortunately not with the same passion. Just for a moment, try and recall the theme song from the hit TV show *Beverly Hillbillies*. Do you have it in your mind? Great. Now, plug in these words and it will quickly and clearly describe our experience with ten, 11-pound meat birds.

Come let me tell you a story of a gal named Mag,
Helping raise some chickens to put in freezer bags.
Then one day they were all fat and sick—
Had to whack them all at once…Um, ew, ick.

Believe me, I have no more to say on the subject. The End. Period.

What Came First, the Chicken or the Egg? Our love for poultry actually started in 2005 when I volunteered my yuppie farming skills to help lead my son's 4-H poultry project. We have so many fond memories of Beans, Jorge, Aahpoo and Carl. What a great group of girls. They were our pets—social, funny, smart and beautiful. There were many discussions about whether or not to include a rooster in our flock, so that we could have "chicks," but we were always told that the rooster becomes aggressive to protect his flock. Therefore we were an anti-rooster yuppie farm. Then, one day it all changed. We received a phone call from a frantic "city" family in desperate need of removal of Mr. Rooster. Long story short, I gave in and we welcomed Topper into the family.

For the first several months, Topper was sweet and just as kind as the girls—but then poultry puberty hit. He began to get just a little cockier each month, very much like my prepubescent son. So, I did what all mothers do, I ignored it. (I know now it wasn't the best thing to do, but hey…I was a yuppie.)

Did you know that roosters can get Laryngitis? I didn't. I thought he was going thru "the puberty change" because one day he would crow and the next day he would…well…not. After a while the poor bird just started to look sick. Frantic and feeling just a little guilty, I rushed Topper to the vet. We were told that most likely he would be dead in 24 hours. After looking into the tear-stained eyes of my son, I took out my checkbook and paid $56 for a bottle of pills to give to the rooster. Three times a day my husband would hold open the beak while I shoved these little, blue pills down his throat. And, guess what…he survived—became quite stealthy actually—big, fat, mean and nasty, just as we were informed roosters would become.

The year 2007 did not bring us chicks and eggs, but unfortunately a red fox and the demise of our flock. It did appear however, that Topper gave the fox a run for his money, as I not only found feathers all over my yard, but hunks of fur too. After the trauma, we just weren't ready to partake in poultry for a while. We all do really miss having them here though.

Fast-forward to 2009 and a high school poetry slam and a teenage boy with apparently great writing talents. (I honestly had no idea he could even speak, let alone write, until I heard him read in front of his peers.) "You really should take your poem and make it into a children's book," we heard over and over that night. As we stood in the kitchen laughing about the events of the evening, we began discussing the process of how to publish a book. It was then I decided we needed to create our own company.

Here's where some of our symbolism comes back into play. Obviously, we have a love for chickens—hence, the rooster. The color choice was simple. My son has beautiful, red hair. Red Rooster. Now, I could go on and on comparing my "cocky" son to all of this, but I'll spare him the public humiliation and delve just a little deeper.

The *rooster* is about:

- Fanning out with brilliance
- Showing the world your shining facets of personality
- Pride
- Honesty
- Courage
- Vigilance
- Strength
- Watchfulness
- Flamboyance

The color *red*:

- Energy
- Strength
- Power
- Determination
- Passion
- Desire
- Love

Well, there you go; that sums up a lot. Like I said, symbolism is cool. All you have to do is remain open to it.

Soapy Days

*T*oday I am ever so thankful that I don't have an evil twin, or that my dead husband twice removed hasn't just shown up on my doorstep to proclaim his love to me once again. It is also good to know that my sister is actually my sister, and not, in the end, my daughter, from a "mix up" at the donor bank. Of course all these things wouldn't really matter to me anyhow because I am of course a billionaire who has just discovered the secret to the Fountain of Youth.

These are the things I pass to my daughter at the end of her 14th year. Yes, I confess here and now (I'm kind of diggin' this confession thing), I'm a soap opera addict and this summer I have successfully passed the TV Remote Torch to her. It was 36 years ago that I began watching "my soap" with my grandmother. I have most faithfully watched it since then. It's rather disgusting actually, if you calculate all the hours I've watched, but I am proud to say that I have missed very few. However, I am really thankful I now get to zip through the commercials, as I'm sure it's saving me at least five years of my life.

Today I'm a little upset. You see, they killed off one of my favorite, drop dead gorgeous actors. (Another wonderful pun!) Now I know eventually he will show up again, most likely with a bad case of amnesia or possibly with a new face, but why waste my time when I could be drooling all over this guy tomorrow? As his family grieves the wreckage from the exploded truck, so do I grieve the loss of my daily eye candy. As his children mourn the loss of their father, my daughter sheds her first soapy tears—the loss of her future fantasies, for after all, she is a hormonal teen.

My soap is my sacred time, as it was for my grandmother and my mother; it is a time to rest. For them, it was a time they forced themselves to sit alone for one hour, have a bite to eat before they went back to all the many hours of house chores—baking, canning, cleaning, gardening and sewing. For me, it too is a time to rest, but unfortunately not for the same reasons. I sit because by 1:00 p.m. the toothpicks that have been propping my eyelids open are about to snap.

So, as I doze in and out in front of the screen, I weave these characters into my life. Their plots and schemes, their heartaches and celebrations become mine for an hour. I will faithfully wait for my beloved because I know he will return to me, just like all those before him. I assure my daughter there is no need to worry. Have some faith. Trust that her future flame will once again be lit because I can guarantee that around and around we will go just...*As The World Turns*.

It's Time to Say, "Good Night"

I've been pondering what would be the best way to wrap things up. How do I put closure to these stories, when in fact each one could continue on and on with their own little journey? I didn't really create a self-help book to assist people with sleep deprivation as I first thought I would. I didn't figure out a cure for any physical, emotional or spiritual ills, and I don't think I even offered one bit of transformative (is that even a word?) information. But this is what I learned, and now know for sure (my final Oprah plug):

1. Life without sleep is entertaining at best, and torture if faced without a sense of humor.
2. Stress is definitely a killjoy.
3. If you really want to change your life, you can.
4. We are never really alone and even if you don't believe in Spirit, Spirit is always there for you.
5. The physical body will act as a voice for the emotional and spiritual body if they are being ignored.

6. Ice cream is good.
7. There is a difference between going on a retreat and retreating, and one is definitely healthier than the other.
8. I love my dog and I still hate snakes.
9. One must really look at the dualities in life in order to truly appreciate what we are here to learn.
10. Love comes in all forms and sometimes a $400 vet bill is so worth all the unconditional love that comes with it.
11. The "mid-life" crisis does exist for both sexes. It can either be channeled into something wonderful that will transform your life, or it can be channeled into something that will destroy your life. Ultimately the choice is yours.
12. Again, ice cream is good, but better with chocolate on it.
13. My husband is my hero when it comes to being patient.
14. My children are one of the main reasons I wake up each day.
15. My girl friends rock.
16. Symbolism in your life is fun.
17. Sometimes you just have to step out of your life and run…but you should always come back to finish what you were running from.
18. Chocolate really should be a Phytonutrient.

19. I thank God for all my quirks, habits and addictions, because without them…I wouldn't be me.
20. When you take the time to really understand who you are and then celebrate that, your life will never be the same again.

It is with loving gratitude to all of you who were willing to share this journey with me, that I now close this down. Thank you for allowing me into your lives, homes, cars, metro rides and hopefully your hearts. And if by some chance one word or phrase rang true for you, then know you are not alone. That, in itself, sometimes will get you through the tough spots. And if by some chance you giggled, chuckled or outright laughed, then I did just what I intended to do—change the vibration of your life, even if just for a short moment. You see, when you change your internal vibration to a positive, higher frequency…you will attract that into your life. If we all did that, just imagine what our world would look like.

Peace, Love and Laughter to you all.

About the Author

Maggie Scrobonia (a.k.a. Charlie), lives with her husband and two children in Healdsburg, California where she owns her own business working as a therapist, healer and professional intuitive. She holds a bachelor's degree in Occupational Therapy from San Jose State University. Her keen observation skills and twisted sense of humor have allowed her to take her daily life struggles and create writings of introspection to pass along to her readers. These true stories not only allow her to survive the daily grind, but create laughter for herself and those around her, because she knows: Laughter really is the best medicine.

www.ingramcontent.com/pod-product-compliance
Lightning Source LLC
LaVergne TN
LVHW051655080426
835511LV00017B/2579